RAMBLER VOLUME 1

a collection of writings
BY JOE STRAYNGE

I0224845

UNDERWATER MOUNTAINS PUBLISHING
LOS ANGELES, CALIFORNIA
A SECRET COMPANY.

RAMBLER VOL. 1 BY JOE STRAYNGE
EDITED AND ARRANGED BY DUNIGAN GAFFORD

COPYRIGHT 2015 © UNDERWATER MOUNTAINS PUBLISHING
WWW.UNDERWATERMOUNTAINS.COM

For Stephanie

RAMBLER VOLUME ONE

R

Love is the
universe's response
to its own
perpetual melancholy;
hand in hand,
star by star
they both compliment
and disgrace each other.

I worship my woman;
she's the
premium bottle
I can't afford
and the drug I'm
afraid to take
but the edge calls
and I'll sacrifice
everything just
to have her
catch me on my way
down.

Molecular wonder;
the small things
that intrigue me
are the things
that keep me breathing,
like little bees
hopping from
flower to flower
blessing the
nectar with
their passion.

You wanted bliss
but I had nothing
more to offer
than a sack of
roughed up
jewels
that only you
could make
sparkle like
shooting star fireworks
in the early morning sky.

There were strokes
of domestication in
her sophisticated eyes
but a nomadic urge
in her voice told me
the universe imported
freedom and all we
needed to do was
purchase the ticket
to live in its
magnificence.

The only category anyone
should ever be placed in
is HUMAN BEING,
titles and labels should
never be applied
or placed
on a human
no matter how easy it
may be to do so.

As the night comes to a
close and that fury I felt
in the day subsides
I am left to the
silence of still life;
no bustling streets full
of automobiles and
patron saints of suburbia,
I am alone and stuck toiling
in my own filthy wine-addled
demise preaching to myself
about the cautious mobility
of my ghostly figure
and where the next morning
will take me.

The profound motivation
behind her tired eyes
led me to believe
she had given up on
staying awake but
waves persist
because the moon
alters their motives
and into the night we
kept alert,
chatting about our
heavy shoulders and the
strength it would take
to deny society's pressures.

Drunk on wine
and high on words,
I stumbled to find
myself doubting
the very graveled
path I've chosen to
walk but I'm weird
and if I weren't
I don't think I'd
be able to enjoy
the darkness I'm
walking through.

I steal whiskey
when I can't afford it;
it seems like an
alcoholic tendency
doesn't it?
But it's the only
elixir that fuels me
when you're not here.

It sucks
at times but
when you get in
that rhythm
of floating down
stream rather than
swimming up
you truly feel free;
no rapids can
hold you back when
you're drifting
along with the
chaos.

Life.

I hate that booze
makes people more honest,
live like you're
always drunk
and I promise the
right people
will flock to your side.

My heaven is
in your eyes
and what's funny
is when I look
into my own
eyes all I see
is Dante's
nine circles of Hell;
save me love,
please save me.

My mornings
are afternoons;
I wake choking
on my own fumes,
coughing and gasping
for air because
I smoke too much
but that panic
never seems to show
its ugly face
when I open
my eyes and see you
clothing yourself
from the dazzling
night before,
you're up and ready
to greet the world
with that holy grace
before I've even
seen the sun.

I tattooed a star
on my thumb bone
with a terrible
 needle and some
calligraphy ink,
it was never meant
to have any meaning
but now as it fades
it reminds me
that stars burn out
over time and I
have to fight hard
to keep on shining.

Speak up you sad,
silent dogs of
night,
I hear you howling
at the moon
effortlessly
and I hear the
cackles around the world;
drunk voices
and bad choices
barreling out from
the vices you carry,
    I want it all -
    give it all to me,
you gorgeous bastards.

A

I still drop empty
cigarette packs
at your feet
and throw beerless
bottles in your
direction in hopes
of you helping
me clean up my act;
if you weren't
so damn intoxicating
maybe I'd have a
fighting chance.

Sensationalism is
the medias favorite
candy,
oh how their sweet tooth
rattles when they bite
in and swallow
and spew out the
leftovers onto us.

We walked into a quarry
where mile high cliffs
surrounded us but
the most astonishing
sight I laid my eyes on
was the tiny cracks
in her stone heart that
allowed me to shine my
light into;
she hesitated a smile
but absorbed all of me
and even if the cliffs
crumbled I would be
contently buried beneath
all of her.

I was holding the hand
upon my chest, right above
my heart and I said,
"Thank you for existing."
She pulled my hand to her
lips and kissed my calloused
fingertips and said,
"Without you, I am nothing
but a woman madly in love
with the search but I
found you and I exist
for you, because of you now I
am a woman madly in love
with a man who is in love
with the perilous search
for the heart within me.

I think I drink
often to the
future memories
of people who have
not died yet,
I know the sorrow
that is to come
and to numb me
presently I drown
in savior liquor.

My swan,
my beautiful bird
your wings were
tucked so close
to you and I had
not an inch to
nestle under them;
when they spread
I hesitated not
and burrowed all
of my beneath
your feathers and
I grew stronger
because of it.

I offered you to
the ocean
but found that
even the strongest waves
could not hold onto
the power behind
your passion,
was I ever surprised
when you landed
back on shore
inviting me
to join you
in kissing the
entire world with force.

M

The most tragic aspect
of losing someone
is forgetting the
sound of their voice
in the prime hours
of your existence
but it is liberating
for now you can
move forward without
the haunting laughter
of that lost lover.

In the night of plentiful song
my art may resemble something
that is entirely wrong,
I could be dead,
I could be alive,
I could be out of tune
but I will not lie;
we are young, dumb
and completely in love.

I've bore the brunt
of too many femme fatales
and in return lost
a few pieces of myself
along the way;
but then architect
that she is announced
a new vision
and rebuilt
a freestanding structure
with the shrapnel
of my previously
broken heart,
she mended it so
with her scarlet touch.

You keep me hungry;
always fighting for
that succulent taste
of strawberry freedom
that resides both
on your lips and
in your glossy eyes
that stare at me like
I'm the only diner
at your plate.

Feed me,
I am starving you
gorgeous creature.

I love you
with every ounce
of who I am
and with the dust
of my past bones
I hope you'll
collect it all into
a little brass jar
that you'll hold
closely to
your heart
forever.

I painted my
insecurities upon
her white wall,
they looked devilishly good
and she wore them well
so I wore hers proudly
and together we
made art,
true art.

I watched the ink rise
from the polaroid picture
and a vision so stunning
was produced I merely
passed it off as a fluke,
it was her,
the love of my life in
the most amazingly
unfiltered and raw form,
the true form I
fell for,
that magnificent being
that cradled my
sleeping sickness and
brought it back to health.

A perfect scene:
my hand in hers
rolling down the
highway with
tender folk tunes
piping out of the
stereo at volumes
that ease our souls
and the sight of
blurred autumn colours.

I love her like
flowers adore the
sunlight and I
can't stop shining
for her.

There's a certain
sense of seduction
in the way she
uses her words,
like knives stabbing
the most intrigued
parts of my heart
and mind her
swift and intelligent
tongue cuts me
with such bliss
it kills the cynic
within me.

Secret sliding doors
slumbered softly
knowing their
cosmic fantasies
of sex and corruption
lay awake under
lock and key;
a politician,
like a glass screen,
can be accidentally
walked into without
realizing the danger
but I see, I see,
the danger and I want
to smash their security
with a brick of fire.

She'll gracefully
pass by me on
her way down,
I never want to see
the decline of
a beautiful woman
but death is a
fascinating thing
and I hope I can
join her in her
final hours.

I was wrapped
in rust and
when she
cracked back
the layers
she found gold;
the precious
minerals inside
a human is what
makes them beautiful.

B

I witnessed the
birth of joy
in high school,
it was in the smile
and laughter of
a disabled boy
when we called out
his name in the
classroom.

His name was Adam
and though he was
lower to the ground
than us I could
feel his secret
of higher happiness
day in and out.

I found vapid discomfort
in the chair of
disconnection that I
bravely sat in alone,
a loose string
unraveled
thread by thread
and wires snapped under the
pressure of being
away from people
so I stood, bought a
drink and made love
to the personalities
I shunned away for
no apparent reason.

There was a loud roar
among the daisies
that littered the
cemetery and all
the tombstones among
the living
dead memories we pushed
beneath the ground,
they screamed and
boomed of secrets
we were never meant
to know but they
oddly welcomed
investigation.

You're so fucking
charming lady,
christ you are
amazing and you
make me wonder
if heaven really
does exist
among these stones
and brick walls
that guard our
weary hearts.

And that when I
said fuck you to the
world,
the moment I saw
a police officer
impersonating a
hitchhiker I
realized they
now have the power
to make us
second guess and
look past people
just trying to
roll on through
life.

I cannot celebrate
Thanksgiving Day in
good conscience;
a genocide of great
proportions took place
and we as a country
are continually
propped up as being
near perfect by most
nations across the
world.

Sickens me what we
did to the native people
and still continue to
do to them.

I used to paint but
not in the way you
think,
I would lay
a large canvas on
the ground and toss
paint at it,
splatter
with random overspray
the same way I want
to throw myself at
the canvas of the
Earth.

With love,
passion
and sheer intensity
I want to colour
you and the world
with every last
drop of who
I am.

I watched rubies
dance along
the silhouette
that shaped her
from behind
the curtain,
I fell in love
with her shadows
even after
seeing the shine
that crept out
near her feet.

Dying breeds tend
to fight with
their final breath
rough and unwavering;
remember me,
I'll be shouting
steadfast sermons
across the radio-waves
that you won't be
able to ignore.

Feed me the narcotics
that balance on
your lips like
after dinner mints,
your seduction
is much more
extravagant that
the tasteless
restaurant we were at
and I want to take
you home to feast
on the dessert
that you are.

Happiness was
never the objective;
sure,
it came with
the packages but
all I truly wanted
was to be stable
for a moment and
content with life,
it's amazing how
she can hold my
head and massage the
uneasy ghosts
that crowd my inner space.

There is never enough
rum to fill me up
completely;
a void, an emptiness.

Maybe the only solution
is to drink from
your eyes
and let you wash over me
like a tropical
waterfall flowing
into a lagoon,
clear blue and so
magnificent just like you.

You slept in
past your alarm
and you looked like
a porcelain doll
in your deep slumber,
I wanted to wake you
but I couldn't
disturb such a precious
moment;
you were still like
the forest but
I wanted to be the
wind that moved you
to life.

I accepted that
you died a long
time ago
along with that
cackling howl
that woke me up
as you watched
your westerns,
what truly
saddens me is
that I don't
remember what
you sound like
anymore.

I loved
every advance
she made toward me,
they were genuine
like the exhausting
chase between
the sun and the moon
but with one difference;
she caught me
and never dreamed
of letting go.

Mornings are always
more gentle than
the previous night,
our fury bled
between the sheets
and the beauty of
waking up beside you
is the reminder that
you are the only
person who has never
tried to change me,
          alter me;
fuck I love you
more than a bird
loves to soar.

Balance was never
a part of the equation,
I never wanted that
from you nor did I
try to bring it out
of you;
our unsteady tires on
roads unknown was a
trip worth travelled
and simply having you
was a miracle in itself.

L

Split lips
and broken skin,
when I saw his
photo I wept
because I saw
survival in his eyes
and wished to
the universe that
it would take cares
of one of Africa's
children just as
it did for its
own stars because
if I were with him
I would do the same.

Beer and circuses;
give them drink
and entertainment
to sway them away
form the political
workings of the day,
they complain,
oh how they complain
but they'll swear
to you that they'll never
miss a game.

Why do you think you
are not special?
Can you not see the
art you make by simply
breathing?
Fuck,
you are human
and flawed in the most
desirable ways.

Come as you are or
do not come at all,
living phony is
unattractive.

Silent poets scribbling on
anonymous pages are
the ones that intrigue
me the most.

What do you have to say?
Why do you hide it away?

I wanted to read you,
            your voice,
            your heart,
            your soul
            and life.

Bring me the silent fire
that burns on your
anonymous pages.

"I'm still here."

Three simply words I would say
to myself as I woke up
during the suicidal years
of my life.

Every morning, still breathing
and bleeding before I found
the page, the ink, the courage.

Those who suffer from
depression, just as I did,
I beg you to speak those
words to yourself as you wake
and as the morning sun lights
your face.

To this day, as my depression
lingers, I wake and tell myself,

"I'm still here."

By the end,
my grandfather was
pleading and asking
for death,
for someone to end it
for him.

The years of surgery
and endless hospital
room rents had
taken its toll.

It was by his own
hand he caused his
later misery,
he stuffed himself
with too many calories,
drank and smoked
too much
but I wish I could
talk to him
one last time.

I could have sworn I felt you
standing over me as I drank
endlessly into the night
but every time I turned to
look I saw nothing but
clouds.

Why do you hide from me?
Where do you go when I am
staring into the bottle neck?

I guess death needs not to
be physically present for
you to realize that it
is always a few steps
behind you.

The drugs,
the ones we were warned
about in grade school,
were not something
I feared.

They offered the promise
of a chance at
escapism
and when the
opportunity arose
I fell in head first
and the holy tones
of the musical of life
sang clear and true
to my beaten down
suburban soul.

Books,
not bombs or bullets,
are the most essential tool
to defeat the religious
lunacy of today.

Education is the key that
will unlock the doors
trapping people within
their god-addled minds.

Stars above us,
saxophones blaring from
the speakers in my van;
I want to dance with you
until the sun peaks
above the horizon
and our lover,
the moon,
hides away again
to rest another day
after we exhaust it
with our
excellence.

When you are crippled
by a disease for many
years you tend to
whither away but
not with the girl I see
before me,
fuck that smile is piercing.

White, extravagant.

On days where she
struggles to even
dress herself
she'll do everything
she can to shine that
incredible smile
and fuck I hope
the survivor in her
never lets that
smile fade.

Her sorrow was mine
and when she wept
I felt the universe
halt its breathing
as if it knew that
every soft tear
falling from her
face was another
star dying but when
it saw me holding
her it birthed
galaxies in our honor.

From time to time
I get the scent of the
chemical vanity that
cocaine offered
running through my nostrils;
I was a deadly powder whore
and I kind of miss it.

There's an orange hue gracing the
rain filled sky from beyond my
backyard fence and it must be coming
from the streetlights by the train
station.

It's as if it is whispering to me,
"Experience is but a train ticket
away, hop on."

"Hold my hand sweetheart.", I said to her,
"let's go discover home."

Travel,
the one aspect of our young lives we
feed off of, or at least dream of it.

Every college graduate, every friend returning
to their hometown that I speak to speaks of
travel, the desire to see the damn stunning
planet we inhabit.

It is inherent in our nature, awoken by Kerouac.
He brought to the surface the mad need for travel, our mad need
for exploration, our mad need for experience.

Forget the job you're supposed to get, forget
the money, forget the schooling, forget the
lives your parents dreamed for you.

Home isn't where your feet are planted, you
are not a tree setting its room in the Earth,
you are a roaming human being.

Home is out there waiting to be discovered,
you just need to look until it is found.

In my case, home is where my van is parked
and it is also in her arms.

I hope home follows me wherever the road takes me.
I hope her arms follow me wherever the road takes me.
I hope the van is never parked and when it is
I hope I will have discovered the home outside
of her arms.

The sexiest
woman
is the one that
will swallow all
of your dark-
ness
and spit out
light.

He fell in love, cliché - head over heels.
The past, his past, never meant much to her.
Every last out of his existence was known
to that girl, his first true love.

All of him, once again every last ounce, was
everything to her.

She knew where he was going,
to the fucking moon, and she was along for the
rocket ship ride but only for a moment because
it sadly ended, horribly and tragically, in a
giant ball of fire, the ride was over,
the rocket in pieces and the moon still at a great
distance with no parachute for landing.

Through the atmosphere they fell, harder
than they fell for each other and eventually
they crashed into the Earth with a grand impact.

She found herself another,
him - left alone after the devastation that occurred.
It broke him down and as his friend, because of that
naive, careless girl, I have to help pick up
the pieces of his broken heart

One day, another will come along and to the
moon they will go but this time with parachutes
just in case they need to fall back to Earth
a little more gently.

For most,
drunk words are sober thoughts
but for myself,
drunk thoughts are sober words.

Be genuine,
fuck liquid courage,
speak your god damn mind
and let out your heart.

Her hips are devastating, how they connect
and curve from her torso to her legs.

When I walk up from behind her and grab hold
I feel as though I am not strong enough to
hold onto such divine hips so she presses
her hands on my hands and interlocks her
fingers with mine.

I am strong enough with her,
she's the secret power behind the universe
that keeps me in a complete state of awe
and her hips, as devastating as they are,
are what connects my poor soul to
the universe, along with her touch,
the subtle interlocking of our fingers.

Love is not having to constantly tell the
person that you do love them and use up
the word until it becomes mundane and
broken down, it is feeling it beam off them
while laying next to them in the recovering
morning from the night before, it is seeing
it flow from their miraculous eyes, it is
hearing them with their contagious voice,
it is knowing in your heart
that in the silence she loves you or he does.

Find your heart and give it away to the silence.

She caught me cheating on her with a pen and
Walt Whitman. I was making love to the page
with just as much passion but with less
intensity. I could never give myself fully
to anyone but her, not even Whitman and that
terribly blank page. With the page, I am
forced to search within myself for the words
but with her, the words drip like gold from
my mouth without any effort every time I kiss
her, every time I hear her name, every time
I stare into her deep green eyes - eyes that
remind me of the most dense forest and
once again I am lost.

Where are my Canadian Outlaws? Why do you seem
so dormant? Is it the cold? Is it the vast
unpopulated lands that highways from the border
trail off to?

Where are my Canadian Outlaws?
Rise! Rise!
Rise with poetry and insanity in hand and mind,
break the barriers, fuck the border below us.
We need not the shimmering golden mirage that
beckons, that is called Amerika.

Show yourself, make yourself known, call out
your name across the Albertan Plains, the
mountains of British Columbia, the Prairies of
Saskatchewan and Manitoba, the cool streets of Montreal,
the suburbs of Ontario, the coast of the East,
the wide open tundra of the Territories.

Rise! Rise!
Rise with heartfelt rage and an empty page.

This is Nirvana, North.

E

I never had a dream girl in mind, never
had the perfect girl dancing around
my fucked up, booze drowned, drugged
up head whilst exploring the empty
spaces between my tortured ears.
But I swear you are the kind of girl that
makes dreams of the nightmares I
at one point in time felt like I
could not escape.

A man who puts his hands on a woman
aggressively with the intention of
harm should be sentenced to a
swift and repetitive testicle
crushing by lines of women in
high heels for hours, days, weeks,
months, years and decades on end.

At this point, I don't really need to
see my psychologist anymore but I like
him, the conversations we have aren't
analytical or serious most of the time.

We shoot the shit, talk smack and tell
each others stories - past, present and future.

Basically, I am paying for the conversation.

I bought a friend for an hour every two
weeks and it is definitely cheaper
than paying for a hooker,
at least it lasts an hour longer that it
would with said hooker.

I was never a believer in the
idea of holding people up on
a pedestal but you my dear
have been placed on the most
high shelf and as the days
pass it seems as if I have
to continue construction on
more shelves simply because
you continue to raise the
bar in every way possible,
every god damn alluring way.

The true poetry I read is located in the
dimples on her lower back, on her palms,
underneath her painted fingernails, in
the cracks between her teeth, in the pores
of her skin, her thighs, knees, toes,
shoulders, hips and every last bit of her
anatomy.

There is a haiku, a novel, a sonnet, rhyme
and reason, meter, characters, words and
sentences worth reading over and over again.

Anarchy is meant to be
momentary,
from chaos,
like the laws of the
universe,
will come order.

We, as a species, are
no different.

The greatest changes
in our history have come
from rebellion and
disobedience.

Life is my muse;
women,
men,
places,
times,
experiences,
smiles,
laughs,
tears,
self-loathing,
self-appreciation,
alcohol,
cunt,
cock,
drugs,
mountains and hills,
lakes and seas,
sky and clouds,
cosmos above,
lava below,
bright sunglasses,
dark and story days,
weather,
settings,
forks, knives, spoons,
plates, and food upon it,
water, water, water.

Life is my muse.

If you walked around with
headphones on
long enough
you'll forget what
the city sounds like.

What a cruel way to live.

We need less people
trying to make millions
and more people
trying to make change.

The greatest minds
end it on their own terms.
They fear not death
but life becoming dull and obsolete.
The obscure and abstract becomes plain,
the weird becomes the norm
and there becomes no longer room to laugh.

In death their mind becomes immortal
through what they leave behind,
what their minds created for the world.

The greatest minds give it their all for you
and pull the plug
when they choose to.

Sometimes the ones who make you laugh
the most
have the toughest time
laughing themselves.

She inspires me like
the ocean view from a Tuscan Villa.

Waves crashing, who she is,
against the shore, who I am,
rolling back
with ebb and flow
gracefully.

The wake and bubbles left from
the crash of the wave against the shore
are like lines on a page
waiting for me
to put letters into words into sentences
into paragraphs into chapters into novels.

The story I'm looking for is on
the crest of a wave.

This is for the damaged ones;
the broken and beaten down,
the lost and hopeless,
the old couples and young lovers,
the dying children,
the living adults,
the man on the corner
selling newspapers,
the fast food worker,
the garbage man,
the CEO and employees,
the politicians and voters,
the drug addicts
and drinks,
the pretty girls
and fat guys.

This is for you.

All of these words.

All of this emotion.

We are all damaged in one way
or another.

Embrace it rather than hiding it.

We sat on the patio of a country bar
miles away from home with darkness
surrounding everything
people watching.

"Look at the men hopelessly chasing tail
and the women trying to find the love of
their lives here," I said, "you can't find
the love of your life at a bar."

You turned to me and said, "Wait a minute."

I stopped you, kissed you and responded,
"I didn't meet you at a bar."

I hadn't told you I loved you yet
but that was exactly I was implying.

I hope you caught on.

We are
scientists
trying to prove
the theoretical chaos
that breeds and bleeds
from the beautiful
supernovas
exploding
from the love
within our
mad little
hearts.

I'd like to
superimpose my body
on yours,
melt into every
crack and become
whole again
like I was before
the chemical
imbalance kicked
in way back when.

R

Conversation was a fire
borne into my heart
and burning bright it does,
flames rise and ash follows
when I speak with people
and listen, really listen,
to what they have to say.

I'm investing all I have
into correspondents
with creatures
that nomadically
roam the radio waves
of life.

I want real, raw
existence. I want to
be on my death bed
yelling, "Fuck that
was good."

My credit card is
over the limit,
I can barely afford
gas let alone booze
or cigarettes,
foods not an issue,
neither is water.

Barely have a job,
student like
and the screen of
my phone is cracked
but I am happy
for one reason
and only one reason;
I've got more than
what a lot of people
do have and I wish
I could give it all
away to those who
desperately need it
more than
I do.

The lost art of being you
is an art I wish more
humans would hold onto,
you should hang at the
finest galleries of the
world,
be remembered by the eyes
of the people around you
and prove the critics
wrong constantly.

You are art and
I hope you
never lose
sight of
that.

The quiet ones who
spend their time
finding themselves
within,
I want to spit you
through a spectrum
and watch the
rainbow that you
are change the
perspective of
the entire world.

The true
terrorists are
the ones behind
your television
screens crying
and screaming
about patriotism,

I want the
science that
made you to explain
the immense art you
create with all of
your living and then
I will know what
wonder truly is.

She loved me
enough to shake
the devils off
my shoulders and
enough to see the
angels residing
within my heart.

I saw her cry for
the first time after
a bottle of wine
and a conversation
about the devils of
our past,
what made me smile
was the notion that
we'd share angels
in the future.

She held eternity
under her skirt
and I wanted
to live forever
but when I
melted in between
her thighs I
realized dying
with her is a
much more
gorgeous thing.

I still smoke until
my head spins like
the Earth but much
faster,
all I want is a rush,
something that reminds
me of the feeling
I receive when I
drop next to you
into the ocean of
my sheets where
our love is waves
beating our hears
on and on and on.

And I promise
to love you like an
actor loves his play,
like a violinist
loves her orchestra,
like an architect
loves his construction
and like a king
loves his gold.

Be my final act,
my crescendo,
structure
and greatest treasure,
I promise
I will do the exact
and precise same for you.

I prefer to sleep
during the day
only because I
am far too in love
with the stars
that watch over me
and I don't want them
to think that
I am cheating on
them with
the sun.

You are the words
I struggle to spell
and the novels I
dream of writing,
the pages I flip
through and
the letters
I wish to send.

The moments between
departure and arrival
are what excite me
the most.

I saw her lip quiver
slightly but enough that
it was noticeable to
anyone within distance.

She was about to
accidentally add a small
amount of salt to the
coffee below her on the
table where we were seated.

"This coffee is cold but
not as cold as my heart
and you don't deserve
how I will break yours."
She said.

Salt to coffee.

I'd drown in salt
just to hear her sweet
voice confess such things
to my timid ears again.

My hand shakes
quite a bit
from the over-caffeinated
diet pills I take,
I always wanted to
be skinnier than I am
and what saddens me
is that the world
never seems to talk
about the image issues
that men have as well.

VOL. 1

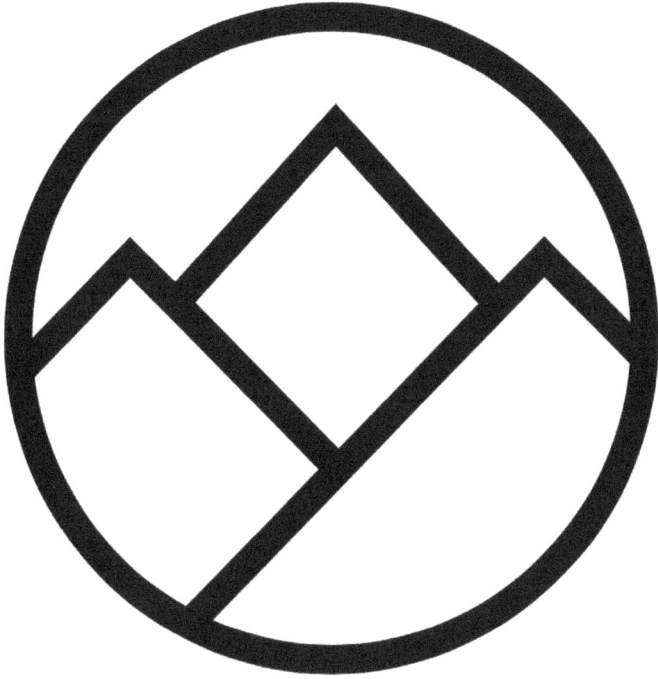

Underwater Mountains Publishing.
Elias Joseph Mennealy & Ryan Christopher Lutfalah.
A Private Company.

www.ingramcontent.com/pod-product-compliance
Lightning Source LLC
Chambersburg PA
CBHW021148090426
42740CB00008B/993